The Last to the Party

THE
LAST
TO
THE
PARTY

CHUQIAO YANG

icehouse poetry

Edited by Michael Prior.
Cover and page design by Julie Scriver.
Cover: *Bildungsroman* by Jr Korpa, unsplash.com.
Printed in Canada by Coach House Printing.
10 9 8 7 6 5 4 3 2 1

Library and Archives Canada Cataloguing in Publication

Title: The last to the party / Chuqiao Yang.
Names: Yang, Chuqiao, author.
Description: Poems.
Identifiers: Canadiana 20230534260 | ISBN 9781773103334 (softcover)
Subjects: LCGFT: Poetry.
Classification: LCC PS8647.A66 L37 2024 | DDC C811/.6—dc23

Goose Lane Editions acknowledges the generous support of the Government of Canada, the Canada Council for the Arts, and the Government of New Brunswick.

Goose Lane Editions is located on the unceded territory of the Wəlastəkwiyik whose ancestors along with the Mi'kmaq and Peskotomuhkati Nations signed Peace and Friendship Treaties with the British Crown in the 1700s.

Goose Lane Editions
500 Beaverbrook Court, Suite 330
Fredericton, New Brunswick
CANADA E3B 5X4
gooselane.com

To my parents, Haiming Yang and Jie Yan.

CONTENTS

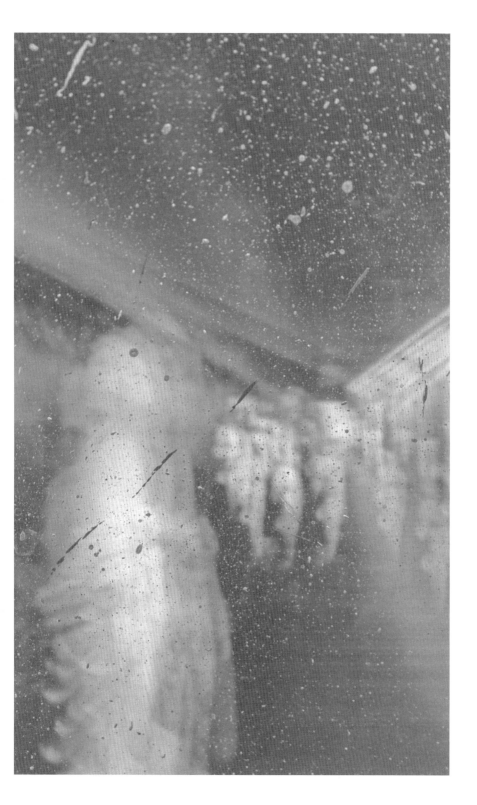

The Party

I was born, brawny in a net
    that couldn't quite contain
the mosquitoes aching to bite.
    One tight fist
reluctant to give up her misshapen
    offerings, I arrived: half a self,
mostly angry, and still my father
    adored me. Pedalling
a rickshaw through Beijing,
    where neighbours
mistook me for a boy, hairless
    and scowling.
Once older, I lit holes
    in our first carpeted
floor, pushed myself down the stairs,
    refused to answer
my parents' calls, too busy
    and convinced everything but me
was embarrassing.

Sometimes I float backwards, ten times
    over the South Saskatchewan
until I'm only kite bones
    and promise: watch me,
a mawkish pre-teen pedalling
    uphill, licked by rime,
peering into a neighbour's window.
    A woman sinks into a tub,
pink and anew in her surfacing.
    I wanted to look like her, found fault
in my mother for saying
    I would. Sometimes I imagine
meeting my future children
    as strangers at some party.
I wonder if they'll be like me:
    unforgiving, cruel, greedy.

If they ask me if I turned out
    who I wanted to be,
would they be disappointed
    if I told them the truth:
that this was the best I could do,
    that being sad for no known
reason is overpriced, that no one watches
    the movie replaying in my head.
There's a girl at this imaginary party
    with a bone in her hand.
I say, Put it back, everyone's seen
    this magic trick before.
She slips into my ribs,
    waits for another day.
I tell her that better days
    are coming. Because they've come,
and keep on coming, as eager to please
    as that one dinner guest
who overshares, who means well,
    but whom no one seems to be enjoying.

ONE

8th Street

I tried to run away

because my parents

wouldn't let me

drive out to Moose Jaw

with my friends.

I sprinted all over

my school as they trailed

behind in a hawk-coloured Toyota.

The dad next door

gawked, midway

through his lawn mowing,

our car tires flattening

the schoolyard's

western red lilies.

My parents insisted

they'd drive me

to the show, suspicious

of my pack of friends

and their ability to carry

such precious cargo.

My mother waved

her hands like two white flags

as I hurtled towards

my father, the other half

of the same bruised apple.

Somewhere down 8th Street

I rolled out of their car

and into a friend's red van.

My father behind me, shouting,

    Er, we only care

    for your safety.

    We'll trail behind

    in case you need anything.

So they followed,

my father upping

the car's speed

as my friend drove,

doing doughnuts

down the street.

Finally, I was belting

Bon Jovi, feeding

the blank prairies

burger wrappers,

summer dreams,

playing at last

the debut part

of properly unsafe,

sixteen.

But they kept

behind me,

my mother frantic

with the upside-down map,

and my father, cursing.

My friends mimicking

their lilting *r*'s

as we cruised

down Highway 5.

At the show

my parents stood outside:

two foreign sentries.

Years later, my father

quietly reached into his pocket

to offer me two crushed lilies.

But I looked away,

pretending that I didn't see.

The Night I Left Home

The night I left home, there were gold leaves
beating in the air, midribs shaped like the scars
on my dog-bit lips, two thin silver lines still healing.

I tasted the breeze outside my window; the oil beneath
my mother's hair. My father sliced a mooncake
and passed a piece to me as I announced

I'd be headed east before turning eighteen,
my wild pursuit of a life worth remembering.
The kitchen light glittering as my father smashed glass,

shards of my family's gifts slivered into me.
My father, on the stairs, weeping,
shaky fingers, absolved by nicotine.

Later, my best friend steadying me on Halloween,
as she caught me, remembering.
Family so apologetic, they locked themselves

in their bedroom, our nervous dog shaking
as partying teens stomped through our house.
My father's fingers holding a spoon, chewing

between softly spoken apologies.
Shards of light, nicotine.
My family, smiling, lifting me.

My family, chasing, breaking me.
But my dark, dog-bit mouth and its scars:
thinning, shifting, promising.

The Geologist

My father tells the story of a scientist
in a philosophy class at MIT,
who wrote a poem for a paper:

I wonder why I wonder why. I wonder why I wonder.
I wonder why I wonder *why* I wonder why I wonder!

My father tells me this, laughing at the scientist's genius,
the absurdity of philosophy. He gestures to the moon:

Now look, Er, imagine that a writer,
an architect, and a geologist are up there.
The architect makes a home, I could find water,
and a writer can bullshit all day but will die
because bullshitting does not find water,
is secondary to survival.

When I am nine, I return home with a failing grade;
My mother shows my father. He cries, he has failed me.

The next exam is on rock formations,
sedimentary, metamorphic, igneous,
their qualities, their temperaments.
I memorize their details, write stories
about their lives. I make the top of the class.

My father is on an expedition:
his voice through the telephone crackles
with pleasure, his pride guides me like a road
until I am older and want to screw off
to somewhere like Montréal,
poetry eloping with my heart.

I am broomsticked heart hungry black,
I am broomsticked heart hungry blue.

My father navigates the entirety of the moon,
finds me in its centre, offers me water, life, a home.

I wonder why, I wonder why, I wonder why.

Family Tree

My imaginary brother speaks of our migration and history,
how time pulses like the green water
in the South Saskatchewan that sputters by our home,
success measured in how still he'd lie after wandering
beneath the obsidian sky that places into his red mouth
two dreams: one that lives and another that speaks.

My round hand, so much like my father's, speaks
in tugs at a mother's hem, as I beg history
to return my brother, whose rage blisters his mouth,
while my mother pours her body over us like water,
my father's hands whetting the steel of my brother's wandering,
who departs in search of a day that passes our dark home.

I grow broader to lessen his absence from our quiet home,
where only the river in its winter marrow speaks,
as my father searches my hands to forgive my brother who
    wanders,
as I honour our family by rewriting the songs of our history,
as I go to a school-ground hill in search of fallen water,
as I place the crow's beak in my slipping mouth.

In the wilderness between twelve and seventeen I sealed my
    mouth,
biting the heavy meat of my tongue to keep from leaving home;
meanwhile my brother sold paintings of water.
And in each place, in my closed eyes, his paintings speak
of our migration and his rewriting of our story,
my mouth a wishing well, my mouth a loss wandering.

My mother is an overstretched cloud that wanders,
while the wild taste of longing swirls in her mouth.
My brother, with his newspaper clippings of our family's history,
with his widening wife in the lily pads of their home.

And there is my crow-shaped father who speaks
of a daughter that slipped from his eyes like water.

My father dives for his reflection in the water.
My brother is a murder of crows wandering.
How to ask for silence when no one speaks,
how to slip through the insincerity of my mouth,
how to halt the night that rushes through our home,
two dreams: my imagined brother and me, halving a history.

Epistolary Therapy

I went to Seneca Rocks
   but by the time I could tell you
we weren't talking again,
   this time you claim because
I'm married and permanently changed
   and because we were always a bit co-dependent.
I've only ever wanted to speak to you
   as if I knew what I was saying
like when I said, Eastern Panhandle,
   crags, leaf peeper, or sulphur spring.
I always wanted to share field notes with my father
   like a true geologist's daughter,
noting how the Appalachians looked like the ridges
   on a reptile's dry and scaly back.
You'd probably say, What a shame
   I didn't pick up hard sciences, and I'd reply,
What a shame everyone prefers to abandon you at home,
   and we'd be here again, arguing.
I often wish that you were a younger brother
   instead of my father
and that it was 1971, on a day where I'd teased you
   a bit too hard because I could,
and that I'd find you later,
   angry and sunburnt, foraging for river reeds.
I'd rub Tiger Balm into your mosquito-
   torn shoulders and tell you I understood
why you scratched swear words into the walls.
   I'd also tell you, Take it easy
because I'll always take care of you,
   and remind you that at least it isn't 1941,
when our fathers had less than nothing
   except fists full of anger,
that soon there'll be a series of children piercing
   the air with the betrayal of their birth.
While you are sunk somewhere Canadian and cold,
   in the ditch of your depression,

beneath a century of bruised cheeks,
        know I have never stopped
netting the sky to find you a reason to be happy.
        Although I won't tell you, I wish you the best
until you are too far from this earth to hear it,
        I want to mention that West Virginia's littlest church
is in Silver Lake, that I went inside and saw clay
        jars full of flowers. Instead I tell you, I think
your brothers hate you, which wounds you enough
        that my mother messages me, What did you say?
He's been replaying pandas tumbling out of trees for days.
        and I reply, What? Same.
Something about their hapless dispositions
        a fleeting antidote for you and for me
as we share in this inheritance of suffering.

The Geologist's Daughter

It was Saturday, it was August, I was eighteen. Quite some mighty thing, even the evening was frightened of me, curled like a dog in the kitchen's corner. I was a little god, I was booming, I'd fall asleep facing the wall, snoring along to songs I heard in my dreams. I woke to familiar hands examining my sleeping face and the shadow of my father's frowning and his muttering, Daughter, you are still too young to notice the spiderwebs on the trees. But I saw the snow he kept in his mouth to water me, and the unexpected tissues and clots interrupting the flow of his arteries, his hunched back the bunny hill on which I grew my kingdom. Then the door shutting, as he creaked towards the morning, a real goner, lost to me until I woke, stromatolites on the window lit by morning. And then my voice, humming to the song of my father in the other room, round and tender, safely sleeping, sleeping, sleeping.

Turning the Tide

My mother's heart doesn't beat to stay alive,
it beats to keep pace for everyone else.

She did not let me into this world until the moon
waned, and so I completed my father and we became whole.

When I return home, there is my father in their bed,
an iPad filled with pandas, the scent of my mother's

fingers, orange peel beneath her nails,
the skins of oranges dotting her hair.

These pieces of the moon, scooped out of the sky,
steadying the river of my life.

One day they will leave. Dust will cover the windowsill
and the music of their voices will no longer announce the
     morning.

But for now, keep their glasses perched on their noses,
the pandas and orange peels on the bed.

Let my mother guide my father
through the sea of their lives,

through the storms of my own,
until I am ordered to return their moonlight.

Lost in Translation

One breath and the sun's rising above fenced lines:

Seventeen and partying, I lean against a playground
wall the night of my graduation, I watch the sunrise and

> (In Taiyuan, the sun sets before mine. My grandmother
> is washing her broken feet, a mosquito net tied over
> a wall and a bamboo fan. She is remembering Lǎo Ye,
> then barely a sprout of a man, who changes
> her name to his liking at seventeen.)

the shape of a friend keeled over, Birkenstocks
tripping over two tanned feet and the sound

> (Lǎo Ye standing on a roof as he called her
> what she would not respond to, until at last
> she cursed and replied to a name that spoke
> like a wet red stone, to a boy and then a man,
> the promise of a husband, the hope of a friend.)

of a new beginning. Someone slaps my back and exclaims,
"We've done it, we're going places,"

> (He empties out a room with coughing,
> leaving behind two rain-flecked socks
> perched on a cane. My grandmother says,
> Lǎo Ye has walked out of the room, he will
> not come back again. There is no new beginning.)

but I keep my spirits up by burying my memories down.
The night is gone and our eyes are hollow,

> (And I recall falling to my knees on the mountain
> of the dead, where my uncles, my aunts, and
> my ancestors wept, as we poured spirits over

Lǎo Ye's tomb, burned incense and drawings,
we were mourning but I kept my spirits up.)

and now tomorrow is gone and the sun is set
and now we will leave and perhaps we will rest
and now the horizon is gone and the sun has left
and tomorrow I will go to the mountain where Lǎo Ye rests

(Come Father, come my old friend, let's drink, and forget.
We pour spirits over graves and earth. My mother says,
Once before I left home, my father chuckled and said,
What more need I be than a bridge between my children
and theirs? Tomorrow is gone, our sun has set.)

Lǎo Ye's voice: a refrain glowing beyond a fence.

The Bridge She Named Her Body

My father once said we are bridges between
our ancestors and our children. Father, did you
ever tire of the pounding of ten thousand
angry feet? Did you too, endure awakening
to a crossbeam lodged in a temple?

Twenty-one and my husband wraps the screaming baby
in a lullaby. Twenty-eight and he yanks her out
of the South Saskatchewan before she learns fear.
Forty-nine and he's shaped like a bell, his voice clattering
against her as she wails like a funeral organ.

Twenty-one and she is the blood of our good
blessings and fortune. Twenty-eight and she is slamming
insult after insult into her father. Fifty-one and he bursts
into ten thousand shards, a baby searching
for his shadow, his voice rattling the gussets

of the little bridge that is my body — Father,
no, you never endured this:
two relics from the same country,
two skies from the same morning,
two bearings pulled from the same bolt

      thrashing, throttling, wearing

this little bridge I've named, my body.
Yet I thread myself through their wounds;
whether in rock, in sea, or in winter's
thick, cold sheets, always I will ring the bell
I've sewn into the ripe wound of their love,

and like two birds, struck and stunned
by the same storm, they will remember
to rise into the sky, where I will remain,
taut and sturdy and ever near,
to bear the lodestar's weight.

Twenty Years Later

All fathers are their daughters' dragons and dragon-slayers.
The mines in Japan are even more cautious now,
nuclear energy is ebb and flow and hazard.
We are going to Port Hope tomorrow,
and I have been sweating like a pig.
Rent costs a fortune these days,
how will you ever survive out there?
When you were little,
we'd ration a bottle of Coke for a week.
God, we were so poor back then.
I will spend my whole life making it up to you.
Do you want me to buy you a house?
Had we stayed in Beijing,
maybe we'd be millionaires by now.
At least let me buy your friends dinner.
Do you remember where we are?
It's Yonge Street. When you were a baby,
I took you down here.
You wanted to be Peter Mansbridge,
but I don't think I'll be here when you get that old.
We went to Toronto because we couldn't get the visa.
Then we had to go to Buffalo.
That customs officer was a cow.
All you remember is that Michael Bolton played
in the taxi, you had no clue what was happening.
When are you going to find a job?
We didn't want a son.
If I could, I'd shelter you in my mouth
for the rest of my life to keep the world from finding you.
Did I embarrass you in front of your friends?
I am not the best with words, with people.
I want to save us face, make you proud.
I talked about Hiroshima, about nuclear energy,
Port Hope. I mentioned that bottle of Coke.
Did I say too much? I know that sometimes you are ashamed.
But I'll spend the rest of my life making it up to you.

Phaethon

I dreamt my father was alive.

Old, but happy, just

as I had left him.

He was bicycling.

Father, I will carry this for you,

but he said No,

rode away,

smiling into sun.

TWO

Trisha and the Wonder Years

Those summers with Trisha
in the sandbox behind
our Catholic school,
digging up empty bottles
and candy wrappers,
only to bury them again.
Her mother was dying,
but we thought
she was just sleepy,
dainty even, as she barfed
up her husband's AAA steaks.

We built forts with sheets
that smelled like sour cigarettes,
reaching under her absentee brother's
bed for dirty magazines,
ate aged couch-cushion chocolates
solemnly, like they were communion
wafers: hopeful for a bony crunch,
then silent and ceremonial
as our teeth met goo.

We watched a documentary
about Tina Turner.
We were fascinated by her legs,
those discombobulated
lines of prayer dancing
into any 80s sunset.
Despite their energy,
why didn't they run?
We blamed the wrong people
and asked the wrong questions
as we danced, rhythmless
through summer.

Trisha wore skorts
and short skirts,
her small belly jutting
out from exertion.
I used to whisper, Trisha,
you're my Tina,
my best friend,
my #1 girl.

The endless lectures,
my parents wanting
more for me,
as I rolled my eyes
in our pea-green apartment,
beside the mutts chained outside.
Either I spent the day indoors,
staring at kids biking
by, or I joined them
in the pee-curdled sandbox,
passing around a Coke
from the corner store.

One day Trisha showed up
in a swimsuit too tight.
Dakota taunted,
You're not hot,
lose some weight,
as he sucked Brittany's lips
like a Slurpee.

Did Tina take that kind of talk?
I waited for Trisha to thrash
Dakota's limbs,
kick his irrelevant crotch.
But she stared at me instead.
I was silent, preferred belonging.

We found a dead robin,
its beak slightly parted,
as if to say, hello.
We put it in a time capsule,
promised to return in a decade.
Alone, I dug it up two days later,
astonished it remained
unchanged after such a long wait.

Nemeiben Road

up north one summer
I licked lichen tore blisters

swam in beer read *War and Peace*
didn't understand a thing

hot dogs crackling as we drove
through La Ronge   passing two boys

their garbage bag of clothes
holding a funeral wreath

one of them sucking on a November poppy
crucifix peeking out his shirt

friend's brother swerved and splashed them
claimed it was an accident

tombstones like grey tongues wagging
trucks trampling baby clothes

pebbles slicing cheeks
Nemeiben Road burning in 2015

Pub Crawl

In a bar made of first encounters, I turned nineteen.
I was surrounded by bodies swaying like willow branches
as I had another drink. My classmates from choir
practised "Ave Maria" while "I'd Rather Go Blind"
played loudly. I wanted someone to find me,

peer into me and confirm I was full of surprise,
promise. On the walk home, I watched you.
Your arm around a stranger who nonetheless
worshipped you. I imagined how it must feel
to be unafraid. To be built wider than the driveway

of his fears, and to be gifted with laughter
that stretched further than darkness.
I thought it must feel weightless, so I tried to play
the part, practised for a few years,
until I came back later for New Year's,

where we met again. No one recognized me,
I became your out-of-town friend. You leaned into me,
and we shrunk back like two cats in on some secret,
when really we were hardly speaking, barely there
except to laugh and pretend that we hadn't both done

this before. Still, I crept into you like a heartfelt promise,
hoping you'd tell me everything I wanted to believe
about myself was true. That I was good, that I was clever,
desired. But you were in the moment, pissing
in the pond with all your friends, wiping

your hands on stained jeans. The drive to your home
ended. Your nails were dirty. I was half-buzzed
but waking, half-awake and maybe dreaming.
And when you assumed I'd come in, I asked
you to give me a moment, then shut the door

and went ahead. We may never meet again, but I sometimes
greet your memory at the end of a night.
Or when that song I can't remember plays,
the one everyone loves that always seems to be playing
anywhere someone who wants to listen will be sure to hear.

Battle Creek

They meet online when she's twenty-one.
Waiting at a Greyhound station,
a woman follows her like a pigeon,
gesturing to her mouth in search of words.
When he arrives, he's shorter than her,
and though hungry, she sips gin and hunches.
They end up on Michigan Avenue, suck peanuts
and chain-smoke at the FireKeepers Casino.
He pays for drinks until he announces, It's your turn.
He drives them to Ypsilanti,
a word, a place she thinks is make-believe.
Through Ann Arbor he rubs a wet finger down her pinky.
They pass Michigan Central Station,
a solemn waffle in the sky.
Slurring, he tells a jeremiad about his grandparents
and their summer homes in Hawaii,
how at least one will soon be his.
He says she is very pretty.
He says his ex-wife is an idiot.
He buys her Camels.
He takes her home.
He says he won't do a thing.
Spotify's green orb playing some R&B.
An awkward torso. His aging poodle panting,
sniffing underwear in the closet.
And when he messages her next July,
she's in Montréal as we are celebrating, graduating.
He writes, I miss your body.
She won't tell me his name,
so I can't search him online.
And she doesn't think we already know,
that he was probably ugly.
That the memory of his dog,
licking and looming,

hungry in a messy closet, haunts even me.
The dog, the dog, she shouts in her sleep,
as I hold her close and try to shoulder
some of that familiar shame.

The Last to the Party

The night sweats in a riverside mansion.
Guys in flannel with wheat husks for hair,

septum-pierced prairie people with western-red-lily tattoos.
Do you see me rolling in?

I've returned from the future and brought back
who I intend to be: reckless as a falling tree,

organic and big-city coffeed, at last indifferent
to your lo-fi shoestring beats. Yup, I'm back,

and so far it's been okay, remembering
how I used to gawk at you girls

from Debbie's School of Dance, do-si-doing
with the little Wayne Gretzkys–to-be. I'm lucky,

escaping at seventeen without anyone realizing how tight
I clung to your bumpers, a strip of road behind the pickup

loaded with true wheat kings, marvelling
at the brevity of your sweet camaraderie, how you'd

forget your unions the next morning only to rediscover
each other again the following evening.

I was your secret keeper, mourning as you left Saskatoon.
Always ready to palm-read and daisy-chain myself

to you so we'd both head off to a place that took us out
of this quiet life, into the bones of dinosaurs,

into any sunset dragging the second skin of day.
The night hurls on, but I'm a mint-cool breeze.

A pierced god of my youth mentions I used to be
such a haughty, ill-tempered, unsmiling thing.

Who we were, who we are, who we'll be.
How to live up to any genuine meaning.

The night ends. I'm only now arriving.
Me, the doughty downer, the petty guest,

the first invitee. The last, reluctant, prideful attendee,
pouting, half-heartedly counting how many of you

are worth remembering, how many minutes are pious
and worth mourning, as the days converge

in a dumpster to fill my life with this repetition
of well-intentioned parties.

The Reminder

Last fall she went to Barrow Bay,
where the cedars clotted with rain.

There she was, beside a knuckled trail,
licking her teeth, reminded of him:

how his freckles always felt like sharp
seeds in her eyes.

In the room where she slept last night,
wine shivering in a glass, she realized

never again would she touch
his too-closely cut nails,

his fingertips protruding
like gooseberries,

the clown who gaslit the answers
to her pointed questions, who misquoted

Rilke without even knowing Rilke.
He was a scar on the tip of her tongue,

a whistling cavity in her mouth,
haunting the rooms of her girlhood,

hunting each streak of sunlight
that tried to show her the better days ahead.

When she returns to Barrow Bay,
she peels cedar bark open, finds nothing.

Each word she speaks
is a rifle aimed at his knees.

Each day is a bird
flicking its wings dry in a field.

When I Knew You Well

In Amherstburg we sat in front of Lake Erie
and the Detroit River, watching the rain.
Strangers smiled at us, two slick birds
shivering outside the diner,
eavesdropping on soldiers recalling old wars.
I looked up to the sky and thought
I'd stay if the next cloud arrived
in the shape of your lolling shoulders.

A fortune teller gave us stories about the future.
She warned you of illness, how your stomach
would one day scar with cancer, how love
would bless you twice; once now, and again, later.
She spoke of a wise lady, someone fearless and kind,
who'd offer you permanence and safety,
that she was nearby but not close enough.

She pushed you aside and spoke to me
about forgiveness. How ten thousand eyes
watched and prayed for me. She told me
I was a menace, lingering on each of my fingers.
That my ghosts would guide me, upstream,
then down. That there'd be no stillness for me yet,
no quiet solitude, no home to rest.

That night you slept, back turned, knees pressed
to your torso. I thought of conch shells,
the way wind whistles through them.
Your angles were like mountains.
I wanted to stretch over you, fill the gaps,
bind you to shale and current and centuries.

You asked me if I believed her words
and I promised you I didn't, knowing
the silhouette of your future would soon
guide you away with untroubled hands.

Anger Management

You are a mouse in the backcountry of your memories.
You are a fox in winter, devouring well-meaning friends
as though they were warm eggs in a chicken coop.
Don't let the Lord's Day cut out your tongue.
Leave your clothes sprawled out like strips of jerky.
Wake to the sound of yourself choking.
Fracture your mandible, haunt the dentist.
Drink water to be free of the footprints in your throat.
Slide down the sloped shoulders of the hill
outside your childhood home. Die there. Resurrect.
Find a twisted vine to hang your former self on.
Slice the air with your middle finger again.
Hiss at the cats sleeping outside.
Spit in your mother's mouth.
Blame her for what you are.
Cough out a bag of beads.
Go to Newfoundland.
Watch the nuns,
habits like apostrophes stuccoed to the street.
You could do without yourself even if it killed you.
Collect words and rent out the remainder of your body
to the stir of bees singing in your skull.
Stretch the evening out by peering
down the bottom of another glass.
Hang a ribbon in the air. Cut it down.
Watch a strand of your hair flicker from
the fan hitched to the ceiling.
Imagine your body quieted.
Imagine living.
Imagine seven tongue-tied
women hiding in trees,
bodies tragically pregnant but singing:
Now you, now you, it's time to speak.

Frank — *The Joy Luck Club*, Revisited

It was his first time at dim sum
as she watched his hands and eyes
mirror everyone as they spun
the Lazy Susan, his *Boy Meets World*
face witnessing tiny miracles
as if a stork dropped a baby
and not bok choy
onto his mountainous plate,
he was safer than that picket fence
lining Debbie and Joe's chapel wedding,
asking always what's this, and what's that,
eyes owl-round with surprise and pleasure,
tasting shrimp, dumplings,
lu bo gāo, the slow motion
of his jaw chomping, philosopher horse
of a man chewing, glancing
at everyone's chopsticks picking and plopping,
as he fumbled with his food,
with two sticks like legs he tried to separate,
unaware that the art of chopsticks
comes from keeping them closed,
god she could be happy,
yet how they differed so clearly,
her mother commented in Mandarin
as he sat a table before them,
that neither party would ever cross
the other's world again once it ended,
and Of course, her mother added,
It would certainly end.

Inner-Child Aubade

So, I find you in a recording, voice
a soft scratch at the door
reciting your father's self-defence
strategies. My name is Chuqiao.
I live on this road. I am nine years
old. I know the way home.
Two days later, you'd break
an ankle running from
a pervert you mistook
for your own shadow.

So, I cradle you, a soft-billed
bird in the reeds of my hair
and show you where we hid:
first, this corn husk, then
the undercarriage of our dead dog,
your survival heavy as a mammoth's tusk.
When you come out from hiding,
you are marked like a dog-eared page
and convinced you are unwanted,
you nail yourself to the stars.

So, I speak softly to match
your lisped voice, so much like
a silkworm's warbling string.
I look at your photos,
tap your round jaw
in search of speech.
But there is only our song,
the skitter of leaves along the road.
The memory of laying your body
to rest beneath the shriven sky.

Yet what remains, known
and firm, is this:

that you were adored like a good home,
that you were wanted like a long-awaited arrival.

THREE

Pygmalion the Colonialist

He spoke to her in riddles, right before departing to China, determined to open an ancient world and save it from plunder. They sat at a bar as he tipped the waitress, who was all eyeballs and gunnel legs. He left the waitress his number and a glance before he turned back to his guest and said, Kid, no one compares to you. I'll see you soon. Then he left, headed east to her home country where he sent weekend Skype updates: China is really messed up, I need to help these people, your country is a tyrant among kings, I am an expert on Asian women. Meanwhile his angry ex-wife sent him Sufi love poems and threats of violence as he paraded himself like an exorcist through a country filled with ghosts.

When he returned, he said he was a changed man, that the plight of his sisters and brothers was no fickle issue. He tried to remind her of how she could have died, born the misfortunate sex. He said, Luckily, though, you're a girl-child raised in Canada, educated, unmarried, untouched. You have a duty to be with me. He held her close, some virginal ideal, a Hallmark Magdalena, told her that one day, she'd come to realize it was in her best interest to accept him, that he could protect her, educate her, make her better. His eyes even filled with tears, promises: Hush my child, my lamb, my queen, tell me of your culture, your people, I will ease your sadness.

And so, she looked at him, closely, those eyes, that face. His plans were history repeated, the conquests, divisions, maps, children, and myths she knew too much of. She spoke: I've heard those words before, from kings who painted their cities and women red. Am I Miss Saigon? Madame Butterfly? That sad chick from *Norwegian Wood*? Do I need a saviour? Do I need a saviour like you? I eat burgers, shithead. She filled the room with laughter, filling his body with holes. So, he announced, When you are less of a fool, you'll know I was the man for you.

And so, she replied, Wait for the day you think will come, when I might someday learn to love you, and perhaps your soul will be fuller. She left him, silent, and he stood, waiting, until he froze into a statue, a relic, a nameless, mouthless palladium, eyes filled with the recollection of a girl alive with breath, striding through a world that flooded her with welcomes; her life a series of inspired follies and his, a life that inspired none.

Taiyuan

A retired opera singer, surrounded
by duck-lipped men picking seeds from their teeth.
Parents with posters of their kids:
180 cm, year of the sheep, daughter, thirty-one in Chengdu,
any animal your son needs.
Held my grandmother's hand,
thick and warm like a blanket.
Two thin women clutched portraits
of their boys, measuring me.
Grandmother, with one silver crown, cackling.
Grandmother on a screen,
stunned by a stroke, pointing through me.
Fasten myself to the bronze ring on her thick finger.
She licks off a comma of drool, I slip her my heart,
a thick napkin she wipes across her mouth.
She hands it back, corner chewed and knotted.
I return it, reminded it was never really mine.

Nanjing

The police kicked away your belongings
while you were selling cool drinks, loitering
forbidden outside Sun Yat-sen's Mausoleum.
I wanted to flash my passport,
convinced it'd work like a stop sign here.
How Canadian of me.
Nine years old, bravery based on American TV.
My uncle lit a cigarette, tossed it into a puddle,
remarked how the sun shivered
in the Qinhuai River like a golden bangle.
You passed us, grey shoes squeaking
with floodwater, your baby's face
a bud blooming in June,
air overripe with people.

Wuxi

Gravestones of farmers behind gas stations,
bouquets of flowers clumped in the soil,
stones without names marking all the girls
wearing silver bracelets,
all the women resting in jade.

The Tourist

There's an avenue
exploding
with garbage,
then a door
to a room
where you serve
massages, tea
to men the same age
as my father.

I am flinching
and laughing
in Saskatoon
each time a Brad
Heather or Allie
jokes about whether
my slanted eyes
see only in
widescreen.

It's 2021, and I read
a thirty-nine-year-old woman
has been burnt alive
in Brooklyn,
as my mother
feeds me
hand-pinched
dumplings.

And like a soft rain
that taps in my brain
I hear myself say,

Chuqiao,

>Let me in, let me in,
>I've got endless
>plans for you and me.

>Why not do more,
>in your kingdom
>in the suburbs,
>in your grand domain
>beneath these great
>and wide prairie plains?

>Why not egg the houses
>of your Brads, Heathers, and Allies
>on the most humid of days,
>and piss on their ancestors' graves?

Yet I shut the windows,
I lock the doors,
I sign a petition,
I follow the parade.
I behave, I donate.
I forget, I forgive,
as you watch me
dig us both
a tidy grave.

History Lessons

It is 2018, and you are in Mexico City.
When you walk into the room, a feather

brushes against the muscles of my throat.
Show me another photo of that stray dog you saw.

Put another compress on your burn.
Send another photo of crickets in a taco

and all those saints leaning against
their stained-glass windows.

Make me a dress the colour of your eyes.
One day, we will do the Proust Questionnaire.

And when we are older, maybe even separated,
I will mail you my answers.

A family of birds singing through my teeth,
tittering like piano keys.

Your palm pillowed against my cheek.
Tell me again of your friends.

Mimic your Basenji's croon once more.
Show me your favourite streets,

the quiet places where you find peace.
Sulk with me, scheme with me, but never go.

No sight worth seeing without
the tilt of your head, returning a smile.

No night worth beginning without
your hummingbird breaths lifting me into sleep.

Icarus

I longed to be the moisture on his body.

And for a time, he enjoyed my hospitality.

We went around Beijing, carrying red lanterns,

dragons parading through my streets,

in the Year of the Tiger,

the Year of the Sheep.

We watched Chinese cinema,

and I tried to be as complicated

as my country's history.

What loomed ahead of him, I couldn't see.

What stood behind him, I wished remained me.

Sunday is always the sound of the door shutting.

Once, he asked me, Do you remember if I was happy?

I had an answer, he wasn't listening.

He flew with the birds,

executive class on a Boeing.

What happens to our false notes, our falsettos,

the voice of something young and deeply ourselves,

becoming an echo, the left-behind, straying sounds

that empty and disappear?

I ask myself but hear nothing.

Postcards from the South

1.

Sneezed into the magnolia's centre.
Host ticked her head each time she talked.
Stood beside the Mississippi River,
a tense rifle pushing through the trees.
This way to a breakfast. This way to a cemetery.
Oil portrait of the host's great-great aunt,
her basset hound's yeasty ear.
Deck painted bluebonnet to ward off ghosts.
Someone's southern father overwatering roses.
Ritz Crackers in a goblet. My ring finger bone dry.
I clenched a flower, closed it in a book.
I left to say I'd been. Here, this postcard
in a closet of webbed wedding dresses,
crumpled in Sunday's quivering fist
of crushed corollae.

2.

The Morgantown shopkeepers say hello in between
Cheez Whiz and bologna. Two tall, white-housed Americans

from Louisiana in their store at the top of the hill. A man,
     teasing,
asks if I'm a good Chinese. Wife peels a sunflower seed.

Quip: I ain't no commie. They chuckle, touch my arm. I open,
     wide
as a new, fresh child. Their cold skin. Their imminent partings.

Man asks if we're married.
I say, We will be. Add, But what would you do,

if we weren't? Wife stuffs him with a sandwich, says,
We'd have minded our damn business.

Trail behind, think I see my grandfather's ghost frowning.
Buy the wife's big hunting coat,

find a clot of white hair in a pocket.
Say, I think I'll be back. Say, I think I mean it.

3.

The sign in the San Antonio Japanese Tea Garden explains
it started off Japanese, turned Chinese,
then went back to being Japanese.

There's a throng of kids with bags
of Wonder Bread crowding the pond
as they lure the koi to the surface.

Fishy, thick lips puckering in the air
in search of crumbs. I want to push the boy
hogging the view into the pond.

But his mother looks
too much like me: creased in apology,
wild eyed, expecting an emergency.

4.

The B & B owner in Jackson said our kind of young folk

gave him hope in the America we were leaving.

The balding guide at the Capitol Building somehow moved me,

teapot lips whistling about her New England family history.

Pocketed her as a souvenir but for what, I can't remember.

Texted a friend, I think I had a good time. She was disappointed.

Still, gave her a scarf from Texas for her birthday.

Saw her caped in it like a hero through Montréal with a scone.

Almost commented she looked like someone I met down south,

whose indignation looked good on her too,

> but I hit *Like* on her post and try to accept

> that the cracking screen isn't her head.

Pompeii

The Lupanar walls speak of a woman:
her art was intercourse.
Here, once, she left lovers to quiet deaths
on hard beds, sharp edges softened,
vestiges of a century of pleasure.
A caged, beautiful bird of prey, a tourist imagines.
But you'd almost think the walls spoke
of a woman whose art was praying,
back turned to a man, knees bent,
body arched, god-searching.
A brave, dying bird of prayer.
Colours, clay, heat, Pompeii's countryside
burning down her body, the walls speaking
of a woman whose art was pleasure;
exhalations come a long way,
remnants of her existence,
her worship painted on the walls,
les petites morts in the history of lost lives,
little deaths in the history of survival.

Grounding Technique

Five sights to blind:
>A knot of clothesline to be undone.
>A fingernail at the bottom of a breadbasket.
>A crumb dropped in Wednesday morning's sink.
>A neighbour's pick chipping ice.
>A cat's hind legs unspooling a stilled mouse.

Four touches to stun:
>Cold water rinsing the fish's spine.
>Hot fever on the roof of a mouth.
>A sliver pulled from a child's hand.
>Dewy fingers in a rotting apple's core.

Three sounds to quiet:
>Bones of the dying neighbour creaking.
>Mutters of a man folding closed the news.
>Clicking of the jaw unhinging in an apology.

Two scents to fume:
>Resin from the juniper staining my sleeve.
>Cloves and sage from the carcass of leftovers.

One taste to feed:
>My stale breath, at last released and returned to me.

Ghost Flower

Desert settles in my eyes.
Blinded, I wish for a glass of water.
I can barely feel the scarf
tightening around the world.

Someone says, Daughter
even the wind runs from falling.
Outside, leaves curl, flicker, leave.
Wind licking everything into green.

FOUR

The View

We're at a dinner looking fish-eyed outside,
bricked into each other like a neat little house.
Someone shudders with news of their ruptured
heartbreak. It's either 2007 or 2012
and I'm carrying the weight of knowing
how that feels. But I don't want to pour myself
into another glass, only to be told my suffering
tastes the same. Now it's 2022
and we were twenty-one a long time ago, sucking in
as much of the world's cooked air as we could
before it burnt us. I don't speak to anyone
I used to know. But in my head, they remain,
a beckoning twist of limbs, pilfered smokes.
Those perfumed bookkeepers I met
in the bathrooms of my past,
who'll never check back to see
if I've made good on my promises to do better.
None of this will stop someone
I've forgotten from thinking of me.
Or someone who wounded me
from possibly now being married, or settled.
Or worse, happy.
Someone I love could be wrought with envy.
Someone I hate could have an adoring baby.
But what is the point, knowing that time,
like daylight, always returns to remind you
to dust the memories in your palm?
What is this gift of finally belonging,
if not returning the tender smile back
to those faded faces
who were quietly waiting for you
to see them as they always were
for the very first time?

Raspberries

I walked by a woman today who smelled like jam.
Abby, a childhood friend, showed me
where the wild raspberries grew, wiry and sour on a hedge
in a neighbour's yard. We'd sneak there in the summer,
press hairy rubies into our hands until we were itchy and raw.
We glowered at nuns in their comings and goings from the
    church,
and I wondered if there was a devotion holier than that for God,
and if surrender in awe of one's holy love was a sign
of strength, or if surrender, like a vice, was weakness
    manifested.
For two years I went to a Catholic school.
Many times, I could have lied to the nuns that I, too, felt their
    devotion,
and I'd have been forgiven for my lies many times more.
I fell for a boy named Olu who threw me off a swing.
I wanted to be selfless in the image of Christ,
gave art lessons to my friends, tried not to want anything.
I pushed a girl's mouth into a fountain until her lip bled.
I threw crumbs on the classroom floor and commanded a boy
    to eat.
I chased a cat down an alley, watched it skid along ice,
its tail like a question mark.
I wanted to be every baptised classmate,
even Abby, whose father beat her.
I wanted to taste altar bread, to be like them.
Many times, I could have lied to the priests
that I was baptised, and been forgiven for my lies
many times more. On the rosewood bench
I'd rest in prayer. My knees would itch,
sometimes they'd bruise. I hungered, I longed,
I balked at the thought of a life without the full,
brute strength of desire. Yet within me there was
always a hatred, brewing. I learned Abby's parents
married within four months of meeting, that they
bickered as they honeymooned at a lake

without a name. Me, I only know that after I was born
I was always screaming.
I gorge still on so many raspberries.
My throat swells, I am aching.
The hope I reach for is without meaning.
I have questions I am too afraid to face.
And many times, I could have lied to myself
that I held the answers, but I'd still be here all the same.

Art Therapy with a Squirrel

A childhood chant taught me
I was egg faced. An honest friend said, See, here, my nose
is a journey and yours, a low road. Later, she'd thrive,
a decent lyricist in a bad band. I pinched my nose to a
    clothesline,
prayed for cartilage and remained much the same:
pancake flat, crooked, seething.
The therapist, hands like a squirrel, advised,
It's time to forgive. But I am Childhood:
petty and stuck — if I forgive, what will be left to hold?

So, I draw: two still people, hairless and embracing,
facedown in a ditch, dead. Name it "Self-Portrait."
The squirrel squeaks and I flip her off,
pelt an acorn at her head. I grind a hole into the paper,
plug it in with the faces of everyone I want to suffer.
And everyone, I'm glad, has passed.
The squirrel quits, skids into her burrow
of curable clients. I tumble through a new day,
write "New Chapter," jot in my secret prayer:
May your children's futures be humbled by global warming,
life tasteless as hard crust on stale bread.
May you always be sorry. May sorry never be enough.

But the New Chapter underwhelms my tired face,
and the sun cuts through another birthday.
A slice of cake crumbles, untasted on my plate.
Meanwhile my ancestors' graves thirst for revenge.
But homage is a tedious phonebook of names.
I draw: two lifeless shadows taped to a dog's back,
and me, a milk-stained night. The glittering, white rope
my other selves swing out of the tower on.
The bamboo pole Mulan and the other sad,
tattooed Asians dance on.
The two halves of an old peach
from an amnesiac squirrel's graveyard garden.

I rush out of the floorboards of my life
to shepherd clichés back to their origins.
Someday if I am brave, I'll cut off my ear,
listen to the world in its bruising.
One day, I too will embrace
the hunger in me, even if
this untethered, boundless
greenery buds into nothing.

I Used to Think of Death as a Room

at a party I wasn't hosting.

I'd map out my escape from losing

everyone I cared for but mistreated

when they were alive. On the phone

with Anne, I heard a classmate had

overdosed; she'd been the Achilles

of our year, down to her weak,

slivered ankles. She was raising

wolfdogs in a sanctuary in Arkansas

with a tall man, our mutual friend.

The operator instructed him: Flutter air

into her chest, like a balloon, or something.

But the air returned, defeated.

Years later, Anne and I sat

in our classmate's room,

the one she shared

with our mutual friend.

It was bare except for an empty mug.

We listened as our mutual friend explained that, to cope,

he told everyone they'd broken up.

That it was easier for others

to swallow than death.

I never mentioned that, years ago,

I saw them both, so at ease,

aligned in their togetherness,

two perfect circles

in a room where everyone

adored them. How, without her,

their bedroom was so empty,

no matter how eagerly the window tried

to show us the day and its promise.

Eve

The bridesmaids are folded into my bed
and I'm warm in between.
I wonder if this closeness exists
because we live far apart,
and if this goodness has a half-life
that we're close to reaching.
Do I deserve this life?
The answer, of course, is no.
I say I earned my life in a past one
but remember a girl who told me
she couldn't be racist because
she was a Buddhist priest 251 years ago.
251 years ago, I was probably some kind
of bride and lonely. This life is only
possible because of good timing.
I'd like to stay here, bracketed by
the soft hips of two people
who love me, this makeshift womb
only possible because I'm getting married.
And if I keep still,
this could be all I'd ever need,
these sleepovers in September
with those who know me best,
this feast of friendship I devour until death.
But I see them, changing from bridesmaids
this evening into brides next year,
aglow in their secret lives away from me.
Time, fleecing us of the most unexpected of things.
The morning's arrival marks
a departure I'm reluctant to see.
I look at the bed of resting bodies,
swallow the hot breath of their sleep.
I promise I'll deny what is surfacing.
So I tap them awake because there's a party
to be had, and a future to greet.

Epithalamium

The moments you spend together

will be one long memory;

each day as seamless

as one footstep after the next.

You will always remember

how happy you felt, encircled

by the friends and families

that awaited your arrival.

Your days will be undiminished

even when apart, knowing

you will be together soon.

And while there may be

years so full of sadness

you will be reluctant to trek

the dogged trail ahead,

you will reach for each other's

hand, feel the other's pull,

and you will be at ease.

Friday

We're watching a movie
on a projector in our living room
after a night of walking.
Two guests are here, a decade younger.
They're searching for belonging
in Mandarin, Korean, and English.
You say, Twenty-one and he got engaged,
can you believe it?
At that age, you eased into the days
with a self-assurance I rehearsed each night.
Now, we share the same space, and life is a wide,
paved driveway. A hymn of weekly recycling.
There's cinnamon sputtering from the candle.
Our house has high ceilings.
We stay here, cradled in Friday's endless promises.
I pass the quieter guest a bowl of popcorn.
He chews, piece by piece, wipes his hands
and strokes the cat's clipped ear, who rests
like a child, sleeping.
I can tell he is remembering
his own body holds a small fire.
I can almost remember
how faint that warmth could feel.

Reunions in the Year of the Sheep

For Caroline, Kévin & Yi Yi

Friday:

It's been three years since we've been together.
I've been alone for a while now,
a sad infant swimming the sea again.

Last time we were here we turned the museum
into an envelope filled with our stories:

a heart smeared across a white dress,
a mirror and a snake beneath a sheet of ice,
Abraham sacrificing Isaac,
      — our pasts, our meanderings, our families.

You were there as I fell asleep,
half burnt, against the furnace,
rosé in a painted glass.

The winter felt like knives,
and still we chased the wolves,
mouths full of fire,

your humanity thundering through me,
our friendships more important to me than anything.

Saturday:

Montréal is warm this year,
clings to us like wet red petals.

Your shoulder is bruised from soft kisses.
You say, Sometimes it hurts
when his beard rubs into my skin,
your laughter flooding the room.

And there you are racing through streets,
a deer leaping through green.
I am watching you searching for me.
I am watching your face smiling,
this greeting, the blue months warming.
We are dancing with apples in our cheeks,
our dance surviving on leaning
into bodies, into arms, into shadows,
the rounds of whiskey burning
our sad stories down
as we stomp our storms into the ground.

Now it's four in the morning
and we can barely breathe,
amused watching you tip back and forth,
your eyebrows raised in surprise,
each time you rediscover
the drink hidden beneath your shirt.

On the steps outside,
you ask me where I've been.
        I was in love and then I was a ghost,
        I don't know, I don't know.
A painful time, you observe, then ask,
        What does it mean when someone calls
        you the fox in Saint-Exupéry's reverie?

It means you are deep in a newfound love,
and that you'll try to be careful,
but you likely won't.

Sunday:

It's the Year of the Sheep,
of vigils, accidents, and red jewelry.

It's a good time for poetry,
a bad time to be happy,

but my neck aches from
filling the sky with laughter.

I prayed to be loved,
but I am already here.

Again, the body remembers
what it means to be whole.

Again, you teach me how to swim.

Again, I'll see you again.

Departures

It was April and a syrupy heat painted the trees a sickly green.
Unexpectedly, my mother returned home to tend to my father
    the same day
the aging cat at last admitted he was dying. The night before,
    I lay beside her
in a twin-size blanket, surprised by her smallness, her light
    feet.
She flew my way to feed me sliced pears and chive dumplings,
shuffling in Dollarama slippers from room to room,
tsking and tidying my debris. She was rinsing her poorly dyed
    hair
when I insisted we could fix it in a salon. She touched my
    cheek:
        Only you find this embarrassing.
I held her hand, we crossed downtown streets. Talking, always
    talking,
she mixed up the word *seagull* for *snowfall*, dismissing my
    corrections
because, as she explained, they were almost the same thing.
In a church we lit a candle and prayed for her sister, the one
    who converted
right before passing. Later, the cat between us, limp and
    fevered,
rose for a drink of water. And while I was hopeful, I knew he'd be
    going.
So she held my hand, and we talked about dying, departures,
    arriving.
And isn't it astounding that after they leave us,
you'll never see them again, and how rare it was to begin with,
that they'd ever be in your life. And for you, for your father,
I'll live at least as long as your grandmother, my mother said
before leaving, promising without promising.

FIVE

The Road Home

1.

Sit between two apartments near the home
I used to know. Cat rubs head against leg,
asks me to rub out her fleas. So I oblige,
nails picking at everything. Grey clumps
and falling dirt. Sunshine catches glinting
spit and cigarette butts, an uneven street
marked with bad habits. Everything is a rough,
ugly diamond. My grandmother tells me summers
in Shanxi are dust and coughing, to try not to
wear white collars because they will yellow
by the evening. Cat curls into me, cradling
this stray stranger, pink paw pointed up.
I lean in, smell her accidents, earth, and home.
Meanwhile near me, there is a lady playing
with her son, her daughter swaddled
in a potato-coloured sack.

2.

Welcome home
to this city of gods,
this city of Tinderellas,
this city of dreams,
where I'm convinced
the dancer at the club
is telling the story of my life,
in this city where someone
is always protesting something,

have I earned my subway seat,
my grumpy morning's bleak coffee?
Did I get it right at last,
with my wandering and wondering,
with my knowledge of hoppy beers,
my strong gut flora from the kombuchas?
Have I conquered anxieties and fears?

Some dude on a fixed gear
asks me my race,
and I say Easy, slow.
Lost in translation,
I am bleeding in Shanxi,
entitled to everything,
cut arm, cat gone,
neither here nor there
but breathing.

3.

Kids everywhere swaying like boats
to songs not written yet,
a parent dressing their baby
in browns and yellows,
Hey there, hi, it's me,
back in my hometown,
lady squinting as I rub a flea
between my fingers, cat purring
as my grandmother tells me
farmers' wives are the colour of cashews,
and what's up with chicks carrying parasols
and lace gloves, that same lady bent down,
wiping her kid's butt, he is pooping in the street,
flood of brown, she is squatting so wide
her nylon toes are spread apart,
her sandals are funny looking
and someone kicks her
and she is crying
and I don't want to know what's happening
so I keep walking.

4.

Tess and I somehow went the wrong way
and end up at the nude beach, where a man
yells his thanks at us for the lack of a good view.

Couples half-clothed stepping out of bushes,
where did they come from and what is happening?
Wild strangers dumping rum into soda,

is this supposed to be paradise or am I in hell?
I ponder aloud as two strangers walk over and say,
Hello, we are Boris and Fabian,

would you like to come to our white-themed
yacht party? I laugh aloud, thinking it's a joke,
but no one finds me funny.

5.

And so I return,
seven years later
bumbling my way
through this country
and out the other.
I am an educated
young Canadian
and my grandmother
is smaller than
she's ever been,
hands linked,
as we walk
through Shanxi
for the last time,
admiring the tree
peonies as she vows
to wait for me,
claiming she'll live
long enough to meet my daughters
because she is so healthy.
Shoulders soft as hills,
body swelling,
she is the last sunrise
I will ever see
as I move again
out the door
of one country
and into another,
our hands shaking
as we look at each other
silent because we know
this is the last time
I will leave.

6.

No,
I asserted to a man
I likened to a dove
who I swallowed,
plumed feathers, aplomb
flitting in my body.

Who I loved
until I disappeared,
who said I loved
like it was a sacrifice
and so I replied,
Well now, isn't it?

And there is my father
sitting on the staircase
he built, playing the erhu
as my mother serves me
noodles in a fish-shaped bowl.

Do you know how much you are loved?
My father shouts across the room.
My daughter you are so loved,
my daughter you are so strong.
Did you know the first time
I heard you speak
your chubby face
smiled and laughed
at me as you,
my daughter
born to resist,
said so sparingly,
No.

7.

What's your opinion on Tibet?
Hey man,
I'm just a tall, Western thing.
I don't know what you mean.
But you look so much like this chick
I used to date. And what's the difference
between pleasure and shame
if you all just look the same?

8.

Twilight paving
a road between bodies.

So easily we forget
that the sun rises,

that the sun sets,
as we fall into

the valley
of another's shoulders.

9.

My relatives press their foreheads into the ground.

They rise to pour spirits over my grandfather's grave.

And I recall a man taunting my mother on the street,

shaking his head in disbelief as she paid hundreds

to a Buddhist priest for his blessings and two pink pills,

paper promises to guarantee that my grandparents

would outlive everybody. But here we are, in this mountain

of the dead, where only the living weep, as grandmother

sits alone inside her home, gazing at her bonsai tree.

10.

An old friend once gave me a monarch's wing.
How closely it resembled an orange sail.

11.

Goodbye at the edge of a stranger's mouth
turns into hello on a newborn son's tongue,
fists heaving mountains of his mother's hair
as she stares at the stranger who looks
so much like her sister, picking fleas
out of a feral cat's matted fur.

12.

And in the monarch's last dance,
did she shudder with life
or did she shudder with fear?

The wax coating a cat's ears,
your friend's bum burning on a nude beach,
the lady squatting, crying.

Your father's pride,
your mother's courage,
the strangers who knew you,

your mouth filled with aftertastes,
exhaling as you said goodbye,
inhaling as you swallowed

your own hello, how are you,
everything resembling anything
we long for a semblance of.

13.

And my future is bright, and my future is good,
and I am earning the forgiveness I deserve
as I continue to say hello and goodbye,
to enough people to fill the ocean of my life,
that sways, that swoons, that swallows
along this long road home.

Notes

In Mandarin, "Er" is an affectionate (but not necessarily endearing) way an elder can refer to a child.

In "The Geologist," the lines, "I wonder why I wonder why. I wonder why I wonder. / I wonder why I wonder *why* I wonder why I wonder!" are a variation of the childhood writings of physicist Richard Feynman from his book, "*Surely You're Joking, Mr. Feynman!": Adventures of a Curious Character*.

In "Pygmalion the Colonialist," the phrase "her life a series of inspired follies" is a paraphrase of "What is life but a series of inspired follies?" from George Bernard Shaw's *Pygmalion*.

"Inner-Child Aubade" was written after Oliver de la Paz's "Aubade with Bread for the Sparrows."

Acknowledgements

These poems have appeared (sometimes in earlier forms) in the following publications:

30 Under 30: An Anthology of Canadian Millennial Poets
    (anthology; In/Words Magazine and Press) — "Nemeiben Road"
Arc Poetry Magazine — "Anger Management"
Canthius — "Reunions in the Year of the Sheep"
Grain Magazine — "Phaethon" and "Ghost Flower"
The New Quarterly — "The Last to the Party" and "Raspberries"
    (published as "The Raspberry Woman")
ottawater — "Nanjing" (published as "self-portrait")
PRISM International — "Trisha and the Wonder Years" (published as
    "Tina Turner: the Wonder Years")
The Puritan — "Pompeii"
Reunions in the Year of the Sheep (chapbook; Baseline Press) —
    "Lost in Translation," "The Geologist," "Reunions in the Year of
    the Sheep," "Turning the Tide," "Pompeii," "Icarus," "Pygmalion
    the Colonialist," and "Wuxi" (published as "postcard")
The Unpublished City, Vol. 1 (anthology; Book*hug Press) —
    "Twenty Years Later"
The Walrus — "The View"

My thanks to Baseline Press, the bpNichol Chapbook Award, the Ontario Arts Council, and the RBC Writers' Trust of Canada.

Gratitude to Jim Johnstone, Ross Leckie, Annick MacAskill, Sadiqa de Meijer, Alan Sheppard, Sheryda Warrener, and to the wonderful production team at Goose Lane Editions and icehouse poetry. Thank you especially to Julie Scriver for your expert book design, to Martin Ainsley and James Langer for your patience and attention to detail, and to Jeff Arbeau, Ben Burnett, and Shauna Deathe, for your enthusiasm and support.

To my editor, Michael Prior: thank you for your thoughtfulness, generosity, and incredible eye. Most of all, thank you for showing me how to celebrate and embrace (instead of run from) these poems.

Thank you to Kelley Jo Burke, Puneet Dutt, Claire Farley, Natalie Hanna, Barbara Langhorst, Sylvia Legris, Seymour Mayne, Jelena Miševski, and Phoebe Wang for your words of encouragement, feedback, and support.

Thank you to my wonderful friends especially in the lead-up to this manuscript.

Thank you Max, the Vachons, and the Monkhouses. Thank you, Juno.

To *Canthius* and the *Fiddlehead*, thank you for giving me the opportunity to read such excellent work, and to be part of your communities.

Thank you to Elizabeth Mysyk for your editing, endless patience, and for our years together and for the years to come.

Chuqiao Yang was born in Beijing, was raised in Saskatoon, and now lives in Ottawa. Her writing has appeared in several journals, including the *New Quarterly*, *CV2*, *Arc*, and *PRISM*, and on CBC radio. Yang was a finalist for the RBC Bronwen Wallace Award for Emerging Writers and her debut chapbook, *Reunions in the Year of the Sheep* won the bpNichol Chapbook Award. *The Last to the Party* is her first full-length poetry collection.